The Original Book Of
Ecclesiastes

Edited with an Introduction
by Charles Siegel

Omo Press

adolescentiam alunt
senectutem oblectant

Cover: Gustave Doré, King Solomon (detail)

ISBN: 978-1-941667-01-9

Original content in this edition is
copyright © 2014 by Charles Siegel

Contents

Introduction 5
    Reconstructing Ecclesiastes 8
    Qohelet and Epicureanism 22
    The Bias of the Scribes 23
    Language of the Persian Period 26
    A Dramatic Monolog 28
The Original Text of Ecclesiastes 33
    1. No New Thing Under the Sun 35
    2. Vanity and a Striving After Wind 37
    3. Nothing Better for a Man 41
    4. In the Place of Judgment Wickedness 43
    5. All the Oppressions 44
    6. Neither Is His Eye Satisfied with Riches 45
    7. He Does Not Enjoy Life's Good Things 47
    8. A Righteous Man Perishes 49
    9. The Wicked Praised in the City 50
    10. One Fate Comes to All 51
    11. The Race Is Not to the Swift 53
About the Translation 55
Removed Text 81

Introduction

Of three books said to be by King Solomon, *Ecclesiastes* gave the most trouble to the rabbis who decided, almost two thousand years ago, what to include in the Bible. The *Song of Songs*, which Solomon was supposed to have written as a young man, is a love poem, but it was easy to call it an allegory of God's love for Israel. The book of *Proverbs*, which Solomon was supposed to have written in his maturity, is filled with the sort of conventionally pious wisdom that causes no problem at all. But the book of *Ecclesiastes*, which Solomon was supposed to have written during his world-weary old age, is not only unconventional. It is dangerous.

What could the rabbis make of sayings like:

> 7:15 All things have I seen in the days of my vanity: there is a just man that perisheth in his righteousness, and there is a wicked man that prolongeth his life in his wickedness.
>
> 7:16 Be not righteous over much; neither make thyself over wise: why shouldest thou destroy thyself?

Could they admit that Solomon said we should not try too hard to be righteous and wise, because it would make life more difficult?

It is likely that this book would not have been included in the Bible if earlier scribes had not added other sayings attributed to Solomon that make it more acceptable.

This sort of editing of Biblical sources was not a deliberate attempt at deception, because the scribes who did the editing did not think that their job was to reproduce the original text as accurately as possible. Their job was to collect and arrange texts by a single author.

In some cases, they arranged the texts in ways that seem strange to us. The book of Jeremiah is not arranged in chronological order. We can identify the date of some texts because they refer to a king or to a contemporary event, but some texts have no hint of their date, so it is impossible to understand them fully in their historical context.

In other cases, they included texts by several authors, because they were all attributed to one author. The book of Isaiah contains writing by Isaiah, who lived before the Babylonian exile, by an anonymous writer called deutero-Isaiah, who lived during the Babylonian exile, and by another anonymous writer called trito-Isaiah, who lived after the return from the exile.

The one exception during second temple times was the Torah, the five books of Moses, which had already been canonized and had to be reproduced literally, no matter how inconvenient the literal text was, but even in this case, it was common to interpret the text to reveal its "real meaning." The consonants could not be changed, but in many cases, the scribes added vowel markings to show that a different word should be read in Hebrew. The

Targum, the Aramaic translation that was read at the same time as the Torah during the era of the second Temple, adds many later interpretations to the text: the Hebrew word *targum* means translation, but it was really a paraphrase and reinterpretation.

Thus, it is plausible that the scribes who created the final version of *Ecclesiastes* believed that Solomon was far more pious than he sounded in this book and decided that they could bring out the "real" meaning of he book by including other, more orthodox sayings attributed to Solomon.

Today, we know that Solomon did not write *Ecclesiastes*. One decisive piece of evidence for a later date is the word *pardesim* which is translated as orchards in this verse:

> 2:5 I made me gardens and orchards, and I planted trees in them of all kind of fruits:

This Hebrew word comes from the Persian word meaning walled garden, which is also the origin of the English word "paradise." This Persian word did not enter Hebrew until after the Persians conquered Babylon in 538 BCE, when the Jews were in exile there, many centuries after the time of Solomon.

As in many books of the Bible, the author of *Ecclesiastes* is identified in the first verse:

> 1:1 The words of Qohelet, the son of David, king in Jerusalem.

Qohelet is the present participle of a verb related to *Qahal*, which means an assembly or a congregation; and so it was translated in Greek as "*ecclesiastes*," which means a member of an *ecclessia* (assembly or congregation), and it was translated in the King James version as "the Preacher." It was natural to identify the preacher with Solomon: this verse says that he is the son of David and king in Jerusalem, and later verses says that he had more wisdom [1:16] and more wealth [2:7-9] than any that were in Jerusalem before him — a perfect description of Solomon.

But *Qohelet* is the feminine participle, and to refer to a man, you would normally use the masculine participle, *Qohel*. The feminine participle probably means that *Qohelet* is a name rather than a description.[1] Rather than being Solomon, Qohelet is a fictional character that the author of *Ecclesiastes* created to embody his point of view. "Son of David" is used in Hebrew to refer to descendents of David in any generation. The author made this character a king ruling in Jerusalem, because the book had to be narrated by someone with enough wealth, power, and wisdom to try many possible ways of living and to find them all wanting.

Reconstructing Ecclesiastes

Ecclesiastes is one of the most popular books of the Bible. It is the source of common sayings such as "There is

---

[1] For more details, see the section about "Qohelet" and "the Qohelet" on page 57.

nothing new under the sun," of book titles such as *The Sun Also Rises*, and of catch phrases such as "a fly in the ointment" and "eat, drink, and be merry." It even provided the lyrics of a successful folk song during the 1960s: "To everything there is a season. Turn, turn, turn."

Yet Ecclesiastes has always been a very controversial book. The rabbinic council that decided to include it in the Bible in Jamnia in 90 CE, was sharply divided, with the school of Hillel supporting its inclusion and the school of Shammai opposing. As late as the fourth century CE, many believed that it should not be included in the Bible, because it is often irreligious, and it is often self-contradictory.

This edition shows that we can eliminate the self-contradictions by making two assumptions. First, *Ecclesiastes* was written by a Hellenized Jew who was influenced by Epicurean thought but who found it very difficult to live in a world ruled by purposeless laws of nature—the Epicurean view of nature, which is so different from the traditional Jewish view. Second, *Ecclesiastes* was edited by scribes who believed it was written by Solomon or some other great sage and who added other texts attributed to this sage to moderate its unorthodox ideas.

This edition removes these added texts, so we can read the original book of *Ecclesiastes*. These texts are in a separate section at the end of this book, with explanations of why each was removed from the main text.

The received version of Ecclesiastes is filled with self-contradictions and is very hard to make sense of, but without the added texts, *Ecclesiastes* is a consistent and well-structured dramatic monolog, showing the emotional and intellectual struggles of Qohelet.

Section 1: A Meaningless World

In the first section of this edition, Qohelet says that the world follows laws of nature that are repetitive and that are meaningless in human terms.

> 1:4 One generation passeth away, and another generation cometh: but the earth abideth for ever.
> 1:5 The sun also ariseth, and the sun goeth down, and hasteth to his place where he arose.
> 1:6 The wind goeth toward the south, and turneth about unto the north; it whirleth about continually, and the wind returneth again according to his circuits.
> 1:7 All the rivers run into the sea; yet the sea is not full; unto the place from whence the rivers come, thither they return again.
> 1:8 All things are full of labour; man cannot utter it: the eye is not satisfied with seeing, nor the ear filled with hearing.

Verse 1:7 is particularly interesting because it gives a rational explanation of nature. If the rivers keep running perpetually to the sea and do not fill up the sea with their water, then the water they deposit in the seas must somehow get back to the source of each river.

The Greeks were the first to try to understand nature in this rational way. In fact, the philosopher Lucretius, who is the best surviving source of Epicurean belief, addressed the same question as verse 1:7:

> A point that sometimes occasions surprise is why nature does not cause the sea to grow bigger, considering what a huge influx of water it receives from the rivers that flow into it from every side…. a large proportion of this increase is subtracted by the heat of the sun. … the clouds too pick up a lot of moisture drawn from the wide ocean levels and sprinkle it over all the earth …. Lastly, the earth is of open texture … just as water enters the sea from the land, so it must trickle into the land out of the briny gulf. The brine is filtered out, and the main bulk of the water flows back to reassemble in full at the fountainhead. Hence it flows overground … down the highway already hewn with liquid foot for the guidance of its waves. [i.e. down the existing river bed][2]

Ecclesiastes 1:7 is conclusive proof of the Epicurean influence on Qohelet. Like Lucretius, he asks why the

---

[2] Lucretius, *De Rerum Natura*, VI:609 *et seq.* translated by R. E. Latham.

rivers run into the sea but the sea does not become full and overflow, and like Lucretius, he concludes that the water that runs into the sea must return to the heads of the rivers. Without Greek influence, it is inconceivable that someone would ask this sort of rationalistic question about nature and answer it in the same way as the Epicureans.

The Epicureans' view that world is governed by purposeless, repetitive laws of nature is very different from the traditional Jewish view that the world was created purposefully by God and that God sometimes intervened in the world in miraculous ways that are outside of the normal course of nature, such as by parting the Red Sea to allow the Israelites to escape from in Egypt. Of course, these miracles are not repeated; a miracle is something new under the sun.

This purposeless universe did not bother the Epicureans, but it did very much bother Qohelet to live in a world stripped of the meaning that traditional religion provided. It convinced him that the world was nothing but "vanity."

The King James version of the Bible used the word "vanity" to translate the Hebrew *hevel*, which literally means air or vapor. "Vanity" conveys the emotional tone of the original if we remember that, when the King James translation was made, vanity meant emptiness or futility, as we still speak of a "vain hope" to mean an empty or a futile hope.

The New International Version of the Bible uses a more modern translation of the opening verses of *Ecclesiastes*:

NIV1:1 The words of the Teacher, son of David, king in Jerusalem:

NIV1:2 "Meaningless! Meaningless!" says the Teacher. "Utterly meaningless! Everything is meaningless."

Ecclesiastes makes a point that seems very modern and was repeated many times during the nineteenth and twentieth century, as traditional religion declined: because the traditional religious worldview has been replaced by a materialistic worldview, we live in an absurd, meaningless universe.

Section 2: Futile Search for the Good Life

In the second section (as this edition numbers the sections), Qohelet says that he cannot discover how to live a good life in this meaningless universe. The author made Qohelet the wealthiest and wisest of kings for the sake of the "thought experiment" in this section, where Qohelet tries every possible way of life and find that all are unsatisfying.

He dedicates his life to seeking wisdom, then to seeking pleasure, then to accomplishment and wealth, and he finds that all these ways of life are "vanity and a striving after wind," largely because they are all cut off by death.

This futile search for the good life, inevitably frustrated by death, is alien to the conventional Judaism of the time, which considers it very obvious that the good life is a life devoted to fulfilling God's commandments and to acting righteously, and that God will judge us after death (as *Ecclesiastes* says in some of more orthodox verses added by later scribes).

Section 3: Partial Reconciliation

In the third section of this edition, Qohelet is partially successful in finding a way to live happily in this meaningless world. The solution is to give up attempts to understand the world, and instead to live fully and enjoy everything in its time.

When he introduced himself at the beginning of section 2, he said:

> 1:12 I Qohelet was king over Israel in Jerusalem.
>
> 1:13 And I gave my heart to seek and search out by wisdom concerning all things that are done under heaven: this sore travail hath God given to the sons of man to be exercised therewith.

In section 3, he gives up this attempt to understand "all things that are done" in this world and instead decides to enjoy his life:

> 2:24 There is nothing better for a man, than that he should eat and drink, and that he should make his soul enjoy good in his labour. This also I saw, that it was from the hand of God.

It is such a relief to give up his attempts to make sense of the world and instead to live in the moment that Qohelet breaks out into poetry—the famous poem that begins:

> 3:1 To every thing there is a season, and a time to every purpose under the heaven:
>
> 3:2 A time to be born, and a time to die; a time to plant, and a time to pluck up that which is planted ....

And after this poem is finished, Qohelet summarizes his insight:

> 3:11 He hath made every thing beautiful in its time: also he hath set eternity in their heart, so that no man can find out the work that God maketh from the beginning to the end.
>
> 3:12 I know that there is no good in them, but for a man to rejoice, and to do good in his life.
>
> 3:13 And also that every man should eat and drink, and enjoy the good of all his labour, it is the gift of God.

To live a happy life, we have to enjoy the moment, appreciating "everything beautiful in its time."

But this reconciliation is not completely successful, because God has "set eternity in their heart." The rest of the book shows that Qohelet cannot completely give up his attempts to understand the world, and that he continues to be upset when the world does not make sense.

Remaining Sections: Recapitulation

The rest of the book is a series of sections that recapitulate the ideas of the first three sections. Qohelet keeps seeing flaws in the world—either injustices that refute the traditional Jewish notion that God rewards the righteous and punishes the wicked, or the fact that death makes our efforts futile by ending our existence completely.

Each of these sections begins as Qohelet sees some evil in the world that shakes his ability to live happily. Each ends by repeating the partial reconciliation, that we cannot understand the world completely and instead should enjoy life and live fully.

Section 4 begins with Qohelet seeing wickedness in the place of justice and also seeing the inevitability of death, and ends with:

> 3:22 Wherefore I perceive that there is nothing better, than that a man should rejoice in his own works; for that is his portion: for who shall bring him to see what shall be after him?

Section 5 begins with Qohelet seeing the suffering of the oppressed and ends with:

> 4:6 Better is an handful with quietness, than both the hands full with travail and a striving after wind.

Section 6 begins with Qohelet seeing people who make themselves miserable by pursuing riches and ends with:

> 5:18 Behold that which I have seen: it is good and comely for one to eat and to drink, and to enjoy

the good of all his labour that he taketh under the sun all the days of his life, which God giveth him: for it is his portion.

5:19 Every man also to whom God hath given riches and wealth, and hath given him power to eat thereof, and to take his portion, and to rejoice in his labour; this is the gift of God.

5:20 For he shall not much call to mind the days of his life; because God answereth him in the joy of his heart.

Verse 5:20 means that he will not constantly think about his own mortality and the ultimate futility of his life, because he is busy enjoying life.

Section 7 begins by describing a man who is wealthy and cannot enjoy his wealth and ends by saying that we should try to be joyful and remember that we cannot understand the world as a whole:

7:14 In the day of prosperity be joyful, but in the day of adversity consider: God also hath set the one over against the other, to the end that man should not find what is after him.

Section 8 begins by saying that the righteous may perish and the wicked may prosper. It ends with verses that remind us we should take everything in its time and not try to understand the world as a whole:

8:6 Because to every purpose there is time and judgment, although the misery of man is great upon him.

8:7 For he knoweth not that which shall be: for who can tell him?

Section 9 begins by saying that the wicked are praised and ends with a reminder that we cannot understand that world as a whole:

8:17 Then I beheld all the work of God, that a man cannot find out the work that is done under the sun: because though a man labour to seek it out, yet he shall not find it; yea further; though a wise man think to know it, yet shall he not be able to find it.

Section 10 begins by saying that death comes to everyone, whether they are good or evil. It ends with a restatement of the advice to live fully that makes it poignantly clear how partial this reconciliation is:

9:7 Go thy way, eat thy bread with joy, and drink thy wine with a merry heart; for God now accepteth thy works.

9:8 Let thy garments be always white; and let thy head lack no ointment.

9:9 Live joyfully with the wife whom thou lovest all the days of the life of thy vanity, which he hath given thee under the sun, all the days of thy vanity: for that is thy portion in this life, and in thy labour which thou takest under the sun.

9:10 Whatsoever thy hand findeth to do, do it with thy might; for there is no work, nor device, nor knowledge, nor wisdom, in the grave, whither thou goest.

Section 11, the final section is a conclusion that summarizes all the ideas of the book. It begins by repeating Qohelet's two main reasons for being dissatisfied: the injustice of this world, where success depends on chance rather than merit, and the arbitrariness of death:

> 9:11 I turned, and saw under the sun, that the race is not to the swift, nor the battle to the strong, neither yet bread to the wise, nor yet riches to men of understanding, nor yet favour to men of skill; but time and chance happeneth to them all.
>
> 9:12 For man also knoweth not his time: as the fishes that are taken in an evil net, and as the birds that are caught in the snare; so are the sons of men snared in an evil time, when it falleth suddenly upon them.

Then it talks about the impersonality and meaninglessness of nature:

> 11:3 If the clouds be full of rain, they empty themselves upon the earth: and if the tree fall toward the south, or toward the north, in the place where the tree falleth, there it shall be.

Then it repeats the reconciliation that we should not try to understand the world but instead should live fully and enjoy our lives:

> 11:4 He that observeth the wind shall not sow; and he that regardeth the clouds shall not reap.
>
> 11:5 As thou knowest not what is the way of the spirit, nor how the bones do grow in the womb

> of her that is with child: even so thou knowest not the works of God who maketh all.
>
> 11:6 In the morning sow thy seed, and in the evening withhold not thine hand: for thou knowest not whether shall prosper, either this or that, or whether they both shall be alike good.
>
> 11:7 Truly the light is sweet, and a pleasant thing it is for the eyes to behold the sun:

But it concludes by admitting that this reconciliation is not completely satisfying:

> 11:8 But if a man live many years, and rejoice in them all; yet let him remember the days of darkness; for they shall be many. All that cometh is vanity.

As much as he tries to live in each moment and not to think about life as a whole, he cannot help thinking that life as a whole inevitably ends in death.

Notice that all of these sections begin with a word or phrase that indicates the beginning of a new section.

The early sections begin with a word that indicates the beginning of a new thought. Section 4 begins with "And moreover" (in Hebrew, *v'od*), and sections 5 and 6 begin with "And I turned" (in Hebrew, *v'shavti*, which literally means "and I turned" and is used colloquially to mean that the speaker is taking up a new subject). All of these verses also include "under the sun," indicating that the speaker is stepping back and looking at the world as a whole again.

Section 4 begins, "3:16 And moreover I saw under the sun…."

Section 5 begins, "4:1 And I turned, and considered all the oppressions that are done under the sun...."

Section 6 begins "4:7 And I turned, and I saw vanity under the sun."

The later sections also begin with a phrase that indicates the the speaker is stepping back and looking at the world as a whole again.

Section 7 begins, "6:1 There is an evil which I have seen under the sun...."

Section 8 begins, "7:15 All things have I seen in the days of my vanity...."

Section 9 begins, "8:9 All this have I seen, and applied my heart unto every work that is done under the sun...."

Section 10 begins, 9:1 For all this I considered in my heart even to declare all this...."

Section 11, the concluding summary, goes back to the pattern of the early sections and begins, "9:11 I turned, and saw under the sun...."

Thus, the book has a very clear structure. The first three sections lay out its ideas in detail. Each of the remaining sections looks at these ideas again more briefly: each begins with a phrase indicating that Qohelet is starting to consider something new, each looks at new evidence that we live in an unjust and absurd universe, and each concludes by repeating an aspect of the partial reconciliation—either that we should enjoy our lives or that we should not try to understand the world from beginning to end.

Qohelet and Epicureanism

Qohelet is influenced by the Epicureans' materialistic view of nature, but he differs from the Epicureans in many ways.

Qohelet's advice that we should enjoy life is a bit like the Epicureans' ethics of pursuing pleasure and avoiding pain, but it differs because he talks about living fully as well as about seeking pleasure:

9:10 Whatsoever thy hand findeth to do, do it with thy might….

He also seems to believe that it is most important to change your attitude so you enjoy what you do, while the Epicureans believed that it was most important to act in ways that avoid pain.

Even more striking, the Epicureans did not see anything problematic about their materialism. They were not disturbed by a struggle to discover a good life; they believed that we naturally tried to pursue pleasure and avoid pain and that these natural inclinations alone were enough to define the good life. They were not disturbed by the idea that there is no immortality, and death ends us completely. In fact, this idea actually comforted them, and they said that Epicurus freed us from the fear of death by showing us that there could not be any pain or punishment after death.

By contrast, Qohelet was consumed by the struggle to find a good life and was very much disturbed by the idea that life inevitably ends in death, leaving no memory of us or of our accomplishments. He shows us that, because the traditional religious view has been replaced by a materialistic view, it is impossible to be completely satisfied with life.

The Epicureans believed that their materialist view of the universe gave them a clear and comforting idea of the good life. Qohelet is not satisfied with materialism, and he tries to give up his attempts to understand the universe in order to enjoy the moment—but he does not succeed completely.

Though he has accepted the Epicurean view of nature, Qohelet is still influenced by the traditional Jewish worldview—and Epicurean materialism seems unsatisfactory in contrast to this traditional worldview. He retains the feeling that the world should be just, and he is disappointed when he sees injustices. He retains the view that God created the world (while the Epicureans believed the world existed forever), but he is disappointed by a creation that follows impersonal laws of nature, saying:

> 7:13 Consider the work of God: for who can make that straight, which he hath made crooked?

The Bias of the Scribes

Ecclesiastes also gives us some insight into the attitude of the scribes who transmitted it to us.

After the sayings of Qohelet have ended, *Ecclesiastes* has an epilog, and most scholars agree that the scribe or scribes who transmitted the book are speaking for themselves here. Some say that the epilog was written by one scribe, and some say by multiple scribes. Either way, it can give us some insight into the attitudes of the scribes who gave us the book we have today.

The epilog begins:

> 12:9 And moreover, because Qohelet was wise, he still taught the people knowledge; yea, he gave good heed, and sought out, and set in order many proverbs.

and this one sentence reveals several things.

This sentence includes two hints that the scribe thought that Qohelet was Solomon. It says that Qohelet "set in order many proverbs," and Solomon was famous for compiling proverbs. It also says that Qohelet "taught the people knowledge." The word "people" here translates the Hebrew *ha'am*, which means either the nation or the people. We still use the phrase *am yisrael* to mean the nation or people of Israel. If Qohelet taught the whole nation, then he must have been a very influential teacher, such as a king.

This sentence also gives a hint of the scribes' attitude toward their own work, saying that Qohelet "sought out, and set in order many proverbs." This sounds very much like what the scribes themselves did: sought out proverbs of Solomon in addition to the original text of Ecclesiastes, and then reorganized them all; their own words in the epilog show that they considered this the best way to edit a book.

"Set in order" translates the Hebrew word *tiqqen*, which literally means to make straight. The same word in used in 1:15 and 7:13 to mean making straight that which is crooked. It implies that one is correcting something that is wrong. In Hebrew, even more than in translation, this word implies that the scribe who transmits the proverbs of a sage should "straighten them out."

After three verses that praise the wisdom of the Qohelet and the value of his proverbs, the epilog shifts its point of view dramatically and says:

> 12:12b of making many books there is no end; and much study is a weariness of the flesh.
>
> 12:13 Let us hear the conclusion of the whole matter: Fear God, and keep his commandments: for this is the whole duty of man.
>
> 12:14 For God shall bring every work into judgment, with every secret thing, whether it be good, or whether it be evil.

We can see that, although the scribe who wrote this believed that *Ecclesiastes* was the work of a great sage, he also saw that some of its sayings seemed unconventional and even dangerous. He added these three verses at the end of the book to warn the reader that you should not take books so seriously that you might be misled by them; instead, you should stick with the pious belief that we must keep God's commandments because God will judge our deeds.

Of course, this conclusion is the opposite of Qohelet's attitude that there is no justice in this life and that there is nothing after death, so we should enjoy life and not be "righteous overmuch."

Given the conflicting feelings that we can see in the epilog—that the book is the work of Solomon (or perhaps some other great sage) whose wisdom must be preserved and that the book contains ideas that seem dangerous—it is not surprising that scribes included other sayings attributed to Solomon, to show that Solomon was not as unconventional as he might seem.

This confirms our approach in this edition: to restore the original text, we try to eliminate these later additions

Language of the Persian Period

One possible objection to our view of *Ecclesiastes* is the book's language. During the Hellenistic period, Hebrew used many word borrowed from Greek, but Ecclesiastes has none of these Greek loan words.

Some scholars claim that the language proves that it was written during the Persian period. It not only includes Persian loan words but also includes words that were used during the Persian period. Even the use of a feminine pattern for the masculine name Qohelet is found in the Persian period, in the names Soferet and Pokeret, which we find in the books of *Ezra* and *Nehemia* but in the Biblical Hebrew of no other period.

These scholars say that *Ecclesiastes* does not deliberately try to use archaic language from the time of Solomon by suppressing language from the Persian period. A book written in contemporary language during the Hellenistic period would have included Greek loan words, and a book written in the archaic language of Solomon's time would not have included Persian loan words. Therefore, they conclude, *Ecclesiastes* was written during the Persian period in the language of that time. Some scholars claim the ideas are Greek, but the language is clearly from the Persian period[3]

But in this case, the ideas trump the language.

It is plausible that, if a Jew living in the Hellenistic period wanted the book to look like it was written by an ancient sage, he would avoid Greek loan words, because he and his audience spoke Greek as well as Hebrew, and it would be easy for them to recognize those words. But, if he had not studied the history of the Hebrew language, or if he was only thinking about the effect of the text on an audience that had not studied the history of the language, he might not have considered it necessary to avoid words added to Hebrew during the Persian period. In fact, he might even have deliberately used words from this earlier period to make the book sound archaic, as an English writer might use the words "thee" and "thou" to make

[3] C.L. Seow, *Ecclesiastes: A New Translation with Introduction and Commentary*, The Anchor Bible (Doubleday, 1997) pp. 16-20.

language sound archaic, even if he were writing about the time of King Arthur, long before these words entered the language. It is plausible that he might have invented the name Qohelet for the same reason.

But it is not at all plausible that a Jew living in the Persian period would develop a materialistic view of the world independently and without any Greek influence—right down to the Epicureans' rationalist explanation that the water of rivers must somehow return to the heads of the rivers after emptying in the sea, because otherwise the sea would eventually fill up and overflow.

No one thought about the world in this rationalistic way before the Greeks. This rational explanation of how rivers flow, taken directly from the Epicureans, is the decisive proof of Greek influence.

A Dramatic Monolog

Another objection to this edition's interpretation of *Ecclesiastes* might be based on misreading the book as wisdom literature. Many traditionalist readers consider the book a series of wise proverbs, and they are puzzled that the proverbs contradict each other. One scholar even says that there is a contradiction, because Qohelet says in one place that it is better to be dead than alive:

> 4:1 And I turned, and considered all the oppressions that are done under the sun: and behold the tears of such as were oppressed, and they had no

comforter; and on the side of their oppressors there was power; but they had no comforter.

4:2 Wherefore I praised the dead which are already dead more than the living which are yet alive.

But at another point, he says that it is better to be alive than dead:

9:4 For to him that is joined to all the living there is hope: for a living dog is better than a dead lion. 9:5 For the living know that they shall die: but the dead know not any thing, neither have they any more a reward; for the memory of them is forgotten.

All these verses remain in this edition of the original book of *Ecclesiastes*. Does this mean that it has not removed the self-contradictions of the original?

This objection is based on the misconception that the book is wisdom literature, while it is actually a dramatic monolog, showing the speaker's changing emotions.

He says it is better to be dead when he is reacting to the injustices in the world, seeing all the people who are oppressed. He says it is better to be alive when he accepts his partial reconciliation, thinking that we should not try to understand the world as a whole but should enjoy life and live fully in each moment.

The first two sections in this edition of *Ecclesiastes* describe the pessimistic view of the world. The third section describes the partial reconciliation. The subsequent sections recapitulate the change in mood, each beginning with the pessimism that comes from looking at the world as a whole, and each moving toward the reconciliation that comes from enjoying each moment.

Ecclesiastes is like the book of *Job*, except that *Job* is a drama with many characters while *Ecclesiastes* is a dramatic monolog with one character. Both books include pessimism about the injustices of the world, and both include reconciliations. No one says that *Job* contradicts itself because Job complains about the injustices of the world but changes his mind after God speaks to him out of a whirlwind and tells him that he cannot understand God's purposes. Likewise, we should not say *Ecclesiastes* contradicts itself because Qohelet's mood shifts from complaint about the meaninglessness of the world to partial reconciliation.

Ecclesiastes is a landmark of world literature because it is the first book ever written to explore the idea that we struggle to find meaning in a materialistic universe. This idea became in important theme in nineteenth and twentieth century literature, when traditional Christian religion was being undermined by scientific materialism, but Qohelet had the same struggle two millennia earlier, when traditional Jewish religion was being undermined by the Epicureans' materialism. *Ecclesiastes* is a portrait of a character engaged in this struggle for meaning, with all his changing and conflicting emotions.

In the past, it has been difficult to make sense of *Ecclesiastes*, because the original text is interrupted by more conventional ideas that later scribes added. This edition removes these later additions.

It is up to readers to decide whether this new edition is more consistent and coherent than the received edition. Read the received version of *Ecclesiastes* in any Bible, and you will see that it is intriguing but inconsistent and that you cannot make sense of it as a whole. Then read this edition, and see whether you believe that you are reading the original book of *Ecclesiastes*.

The Original Text of
Ecclesiastes

1. No New Thing Under the Sun

1:1 The words of Qohelet, the son of David, king in Jerusalem.

1:2 Vanity of vanities, saith Qohelet, vanity of vanities; all is vanity.

1:3 What profit hath a man of all his labour which he taketh under the sun?

1:4 One generation passeth away, and another generation cometh: but the earth abideth for ever.

1:5 The sun also ariseth, and the sun goeth down, and hasteth to his place where he arose.

1:6 The wind goeth toward the south, and turneth about unto the north; it whirleth about continually, and the wind returneth again according to his circuits.

1:7 All the rivers run into the sea; yet the sea is not full; unto the place from whence the rivers come, thither they return again.

1:8 All things are full of labour; man cannot utter it: the eye is not satisfied with seeing, nor the ear filled with hearing.

1:9 The thing that hath been, it is that which shall be; and that which is done is that which shall be done: and there is no new thing under the sun.

1:10 Is there any thing whereof it may be said, See, this is new? it hath been already of old time, which was before us.

1:11 There is no remembrance of former things; neither shall there be any remembrance of things that are to come with those that shall come after.

2. Vanity and a Striving After Wind

1:12 I Qohelet was king over Israel in Jerusalem.

1:13 And I gave my heart to seek and search out by wisdom concerning all things that are done under heaven: this sore travail hath God given to the sons of man to be exercised therewith.

1:14 I have seen all the works that are done under the sun; and, behold, all is vanity and a striving after wind.

1:15 That which is crooked cannot be made straight: and that which is wanting cannot be numbered.

1:16 I communed with mine own heart, saying, Lo, I am come to great estate, and have gotten more wisdom than all they that have been before me in Jerusalem: yea, my heart had great experience of wisdom and knowledge.

1:17 And I gave my heart to know wisdom, and to know madness and folly: I perceived that this also is a striving after wind.

1:18 For in much wisdom is much grief: and he that increaseth knowledge increaseth sorrow.

2:1 I said in mine heart, Go to now, I will prove thee with mirth, therefore enjoy pleasure: and, behold, this also is vanity.

2:2 I said of laughter, It is mad: and of mirth, What doeth it?

2:3 I sought in mine heart to give myself unto wine, still guiding mine heart with wisdom; and to lay hold on folly, till I might see what was that good for the sons of men, which they should do under the heaven all the days of their life.

2:4 I made me great works; I builded me houses; I planted me vineyards:

2:5 I made me gardens and orchards, and I planted trees in them of all kind of fruits:

2:6 I made me pools of water, to water therewith the wood that bringeth forth trees:

2:7 I got me servants and maidens, and had servants born in my house; also I had great possessions of great and small cattle above all that were in Jerusalem before me:

2:8 I gathered me also silver and gold, and the peculiar treasure of kings and of the provinces: I gat me men singers and women singers, and the delights of the sons of men, as musical instruments, and that of all sorts.

2:9 So I was great, and increased more than all that were before me in Jerusalem: also my wisdom remained with me.

2:10 And whatsoever mine eyes desired I kept not from them, I withheld not my heart from any joy; for my heart rejoiced in all my labour: and this was my portion of all my labour.

2:11 Then I looked on all the works that my hands had wrought, and on the labour that I had laboured to do: and, behold, all was vanity and a striving after wind, and there was no profit under the sun.

2:12 And I turned myself to behold wisdom, and madness, and folly: for what can the man do that cometh after the king? even that which hath been already done.

2:13 Then I saw that wisdom excelleth folly, as far as light excelleth darkness.

2:14 The wise man's eyes are in his head; but the fool walketh in darkness: and I myself perceived also that one event happeneth to them all.

2:15 Then said I in my heart, As it happeneth to the fool, so it happeneth even to me; and why was I then more wise? Then I said in my heart, that this also is vanity.

2:16 For there is no remembrance of the wise more than of the fool for ever; seeing that which now is in the days to come shall all be forgotten. And how dieth the wise man? as the fool.

2:17 Therefore I hated life; because the work that is wrought under the sun is grievous unto me: for all is vanity and a striving after wind.

2:18 Yea, I hated all my labour which I had taken under the sun: because I should leave it unto the man that shall be after me.

2:19 And who knoweth whether he shall be a wise man or a fool? yet shall he have rule over all my labour wherein I have laboured, and wherein I have shewed myself wise under the sun. This is also vanity.

2:20 Therefore I went about to cause my heart to despair of all the labour which I took under the sun.

2:21 For there is a man whose labour is in wisdom, and in knowledge, and in equity; yet to a man that hath not laboured therein shall he leave it for his portion. This also is vanity and a great evil.

2:22 For what hath man of all his labour, and of the vexation of his heart, wherein he hath laboured under the sun?

2:23 For all his days are sorrows, and his travail grief; yea, his heart taketh not rest in the night. This is also vanity.

3. Nothing Better for a Man

2:24 There is nothing better for a man, than that he should eat and drink, and that he should make his soul enjoy good in his labour.

3:1 To every thing there is a season, and a time to every purpose under the heaven:

3:2 A time to be born, and a time to die;

a time to plant, and a time to pluck up that which is planted;

3:3 A time to kill, and a time to heal;

a time to break down, and a time to build up;

3:4 A time to weep, and a time to laugh;

a time to mourn, and a time to dance;

3:5 A time to cast away stones, and a time to gather stones together;

a time to embrace, and a time to refrain from embracing;

3:6 A time to get, and a time to lose;

a time to keep, and a time to cast away;

3:7 A time to rend, and a time to sew;

a time to keep silence, and a time to speak;

3:8 A time to love, and a time to hate;

a time of war, and a time of peace.

3:9 What profit hath he that worketh in that wherein he laboureth?

3:10 I have seen the travail, which God hath given to the sons of men to be exercised in it.

3:11 He hath made every thing beautiful in his time: also he hath set eternity in their heart, so that no man can find out the work that God maketh from the beginning to the end.

3:12 I know that there is no good in them, but for a man to rejoice, and to do good in his life.

3:13 And also that every man should eat and drink, and enjoy the good of all his labour, it is the gift of God.

3:14 I know that, whatsoever God doeth, it is for ever: nothing can be added to it, nor any thing taken from it: and God doeth it, that men should fear before him.

3:15 That which hath been is now; and that which is to be hath already been; and God requireth that which is past.

4. In the Place of Judgment Wickedness

3:16 And moreover I saw under the sun the place of judgment, that wickedness was there; and the place of righteousness, that iniquity was there.

3:18 I said in mine heart concerning the estate of the sons of men, that God is testing them, that they might see that they themselves are beasts.

3:19 For that which befalleth the sons of men befalleth beasts; even one thing befalleth them: as the one dieth, so dieth the other; yea, they have all one breath; so that a man hath no preeminence above a beast: for all is vanity.

3:20 All go unto one place; all are of the dust, and all turn to dust again.

3:21 Who knoweth the spirit of man that goeth upward, and the spirit of the beast that goeth downward to the earth?

3:22 Wherefore I perceive that there is nothing better, than that a man should rejoice in his own works; for that is his portion: for who shall bring him to see what shall be after him?

5. All the Oppressions

4:1 And I turned, and considered all the oppressions that are done under the sun: and behold the tears of such as were oppressed, and they had no comforter; and on the side of their oppressors there was power; but they had no comforter.

4:2 Wherefore I praised the dead which are already dead more than the living which are yet alive.

4:3 Yea, better is he than both they, which hath not yet been, who hath not seen the evil work that is done under the sun.

4:4 Again, I considered all travail, and every right work, that for this a man is envied of his neighbour. This is also vanity and a striving after wind.

4:5 The fool foldeth his hands together, and eateth his own flesh.

4:6 Better is an handful with quietness, than both the hands full with travail and a striving after wind.

6. Neither Is His Eye Satisfied with Riches

4:7 And I turned, and I saw vanity under the sun.

5:10 He that loveth money is not satisfied with money; nor he that loveth wealth with increase: this is also vanity.

5:11 When goods increase, they are increased that eat them: and what good is there to the owners thereof, saving the beholding of them with their eyes?

5:12 The sleep of a labouring man is sweet, whether he eat little or much: but the abundance of the rich will not suffer him to sleep.

5:13 There is a sore evil which I have seen under the sun, namely, riches kept for the owners thereof to their hurt.

5:15 As he came forth of his mother's womb, naked shall he return to go as he came, and shall take nothing of his labour, which he may carry away in his hand.

5:16 And this also is a sore evil, that in all points as he came, so shall he go: and what profit hath he that hath laboured for the wind?

5:17 All his days also he eateth in darkness, and he hath much sorrow and wrath with his sickness.

5:18 Behold that which I have seen: it is good and comely for one to eat and to drink, and to enjoy the good of all his labour that he taketh under the sun all the days of his life, which God giveth him: for it is his portion.

5:19 Every man also to whom God hath given riches and wealth, and hath given him power to eat thereof, and to take his portion, and to rejoice in his labour; this is the gift of God.

5:20 For he shall not much call to mind the days of his life; because God answereth him in the joy of his heart.

7. He Does Not Enjoy Life's Good Things

6:1 There is an evil which I have seen under the sun, and it is common among men:

6:2 A man to whom God hath given riches, wealth, and honour, so that he wanteth nothing for his soul of all that he desireth, yet God giveth him not power to eat thereof, but a stranger eateth it: this is vanity, and it is an evil disease.

6:3 If a man beget an hundred children, and live many years, so that the days of his years be many, and he does not enjoy life's good things; I say, that an untimely birth is better than he.

6:4 For it cometh in with vanity, and departeth in darkness, and its name shall be covered with darkness.

6:5 Moreover it hath not seen the sun, nor known any thing: it has more rest than he.

6:6 Yea, though he live a thousand years twice told, yet hath he seen no good: do not all go to one place?

6:7 All the labour of man is for his mouth, and yet the appetite is not filled.

6:8 For what hath the wise man more than the fool? what hath the poor man, that knoweth how to conduct himself before the living?

6:9 Better is the sight of the eyes than the wandering of the desire: this is also vanity and a striving after wind.

6:12 For who knoweth what is good for man in this life, all the days of his vain life which he spendeth as a shadow? for who can tell a man what shall be after him under the sun?

7:13 Consider the work of God: for who can make that straight, which he hath made crooked?

7:14 In the day of prosperity be joyful, but in the day of adversity consider: God also hath set the one over against the other, to the end that man should not find what is after him.

8. A Righteous Man Perishes

7:15 All things have I seen in the days of my vanity: there is a just man that perisheth in his righteousness, and there is a wicked man that prolongeth his life in his wickedness.

7:16 Be not righteous over much; neither make thyself over wise: why shouldest thou destroy thyself?

7:17 Be not over much wicked, neither be thou foolish: why shouldest thou die before thy time?

7:20 For there is not a just man upon earth, that doeth good, and sinneth not.

7:23 All this have I proved by wisdom: I said, I will be wise; but it was far from me.

7:24 That which is far off, and exceeding deep, who can find it out?

7:25 I applied mine heart to know, and to search, and to seek out wisdom, and the reason of things, and to know the wickedness of folly, even of foolishness and madness:

7:27 Behold, this have I found, counting one by one, to find out the account:

7:28a Which yet my soul seeketh, but I find not.

8:6 Because to every purpose there is time and judgment, although the misery of man is great upon him.

8:7 For he knoweth not that which shall be: for who can tell him?

9. The Wicked Praised in the City

8:9 All this have I seen, and applied my heart unto every work that is done under the sun: there is a time wherein one man ruleth over another to his own hurt.

8:10 And so I saw the wicked buried, who had come and gone from the place of the holy, and they were forgotten in the city where they had so done: this is also vanity.

8:14 There is a vanity which is done upon the earth; that there be just men, unto whom it happeneth according to the work of the wicked; again, there be wicked men, to whom it happeneth according to the work of the righteous: I said that this also is vanity.

8:15 Then I commended mirth, because a man hath no better thing under the sun, than to eat, and to drink, and to be merry: for that shall abide with him in his labour the days of his life, which God giveth him under the sun.

8:16 When I applied mine heart to know wisdom, and to see the business that is done upon the earth: (for also there is that neither day nor night seeth sleep with his eyes:)

8:17 Then I beheld all the work of God, that a man cannot find out the work that is done under the sun: because though a man labour to seek it out, yet he shall not find it; yea further; though a wise man think to know it, yet shall he not be able to find it.

10. One Fate Comes to All

9:1 For all this I considered in my heart even to declare all this, that the righteous, and the wise, and their works, are in the hand of God: man does knoweth not all that is before them, love or hatred.

9:2 All things come alike to all: there is one event to the righteous, and to the wicked; to the good and to the clean, and to the unclean; to him that sacrificeth, and to him that sacrificeth not: as is the good, so is the sinner; and he that sweareth, as he that feareth an oath.

9:3 This is an evil among all things that are done under the sun, that there is one event unto all: yea, also the heart of the sons of men is full of evil, and madness is in their heart while they live, and after that they go to the dead.

9:4 For to him that is joined to all the living there is hope: for a living dog is better than a dead lion.

9:5 For the living know that they shall die: but the dead know not any thing, neither have they any more a reward; for the memory of them is forgotten.

9:6 Also their love, and their hatred, and their envy, is now perished; neither have they any more a portion for ever in any thing that is done under the sun.

9:7 Go thy way, eat thy bread with joy, and drink thy wine with a merry heart; for God now accepteth thy works.

9:8 Let thy garments be always white; and let thy head lack no ointment.

9:9 Live joyfully with the wife whom thou lovest all the days of the life of thy vanity, which he hath given thee under the sun, all the days of thy vanity: for that is thy portion in this life, and in thy labour which thou takest under the sun.

9:10 Whatsoever thy hand findeth to do, do it with thy might; for there is no work, nor device, nor knowledge, nor wisdom, in the grave, whither thou goest.

11. The Race Is Not to the Swift

9:11 I turned, and saw under the sun, that the race is not to the swift, nor the battle to the strong, neither yet bread to the wise, nor yet riches to men of understanding, nor yet favour to men of skill; but time and chance happeneth to them all.

9:12 For man also knoweth not his time: as the fishes that are taken in an evil net, and as the birds that are caught in the snare; so are the sons of men snared in an evil time, when it falleth suddenly upon them.

9:13 This wisdom have I seen also under the sun, and it seemed great unto me:

10:8 He that diggeth a pit may fall into it; and he that breaketh a wall, a serpent may bite him.

10:9 He that removeth stones may be hurt therewith; and he that cleaveth wood may be endangered thereby.

10:11 If the serpent bites before it is charmed, there is no advantage for the charmer.

10:19 A feast is made for laughter, and wine maketh merry, and money answereth all things.

11:3 If the clouds be full of rain, they empty themselves upon the earth: and if the tree fall toward the south, or toward the north, in the place where the tree falleth, there it shall be.

11:4 He that observeth the wind shall not sow; and he that regardeth the clouds shall not reap.

11:5 As thou knowest not what is the way of the spirit, nor how the bones do grow in the womb of her that is with child: even so thou knowest not the works of God who maketh all.

11:6 In the morning sow thy seed, and in the evening withhold not thine hand: for thou knowest not whether shall prosper, either this or that, or whether they both shall be alike good.

11:7 Truly the light is sweet, and a pleasant thing it is for the eyes to behold the sun:

11:8 But if a man live many years, and rejoice in them all; yet let him remember the days of darkness; for they shall be many. All that cometh is vanity.

About the Translation

This translation is based on the King James Version of the Bible. It changes the King James Version only when the change is essential, either because the archaic language of the King James Version would confuse the contemporary reader or because the change clarifies the overall meaning of the book.

There have been long scholarly disputes about the translations of many words in *Ecclesiastes*, and any attempt to deal with all these issues would be a monumental task. It is better to heed the admonition

> 12:12 ... of making many books there is no end;
> and much study is a weariness of the flesh.

and to avoid this weariness by making only changes that are necessary.

This section lists all the changes from the King James Version made by this edition, and all the cases where this edition keeps the translation of the King James Version, though it might be considered controversial.

Qohelet and the Qohelet

Throughout, this edition replaces "the Preacher" in the King James version with either "Qohelet" or "the Qohelet," a complicated issue that demands a section of its own.

Qohelet is probably a name rather than a description. Yet later scribes who wrote "the Qohelet" in Hebrew and those who translated the book into the Greek of the Septuagint thought it was a description, which could be translated as "the member of the assembly" or "the Preacher."

In Hebrew, *qohelet* is a female participle. To call a man "the preacher" of "the member of the assembly," you would normally use *haqohel*, using the male participle, *qohel* plus the definite article, *ha*.

There are men's names in the same form as Qohelet in the books of Ezra and Nehemia, in the lists of Jews who returned from Babylon. In Nehemia 7:57 and Nehemia 7:59 and in Ezra 2:55 and Ezra 2:57, the names listed include "Soferet" and "Pocheret of Zebaim." But even here, there is confusion: there is a glaring difference in the lists of names in the following two verses:

> Nehemia 7:57 the children of Solomon's servants: … the children of Soferet …. (Hebrew: *soferet*)

> Ezra 2:55 the children of Solomon's servants: … the children of the Soferet …. (Hebrew: *hasoferet*)

We see the same confusion as we see in *Ecclesiastes*, which uses both *qohelet* and *haqohelet* ("the *qohelet*"). Nehemia uses *soferet* and Ezra uses *hasoferet* ("the *soferet*").

One possible explanation is that *soferet* and *pocheret* were ritual offices that were invented when the Jews were in Babylon, when they began to speak Aramaic rather than Hebrew. *Soferet* is the female version of *sofer*, which means scribe, and it is plausible that there was some new religious function of scribe in exile, and that they gave this new function a new name in the feminine form to distinguish it from ordinary scribes. Later, men might have been given names based on this function, just as English gave men names like Smith or Farmer based on their occupation.

Grammatically, "Qohelet" would be used as a name and "the qohelet" would be used to refer to the office, just as we use "Smith" as a name and "the smith" as the position. In Hebrew, there is no indefinite article, so *qohelet* can also mean "a qohelet," but *Ecclesiastes* is obviously referring to a specific person, so the office with an indefinite article is not relevant here.

Thus, it seems plausible that "Qohelet" should be used as a name (like "Smith"), while "the qohelet" should be used to refer to someone based on his position (like "the smith"). We cannot be certain of this, given the confused use of "the soferet" as a name in Ezra 2:55, but it is a reasonable working hypothesis.

Based on this hypothesis, the fact that the speaker is sometimes called "Qohelet" and sometimes "the qohelet" also reveals something about the way that scribes transmitted this book.

When the speaker refers to himself, he uses "qohelet" rather than "the qohelet":

> 1:12 I Qohelet was king over Israel in Jerusalem.

This verse seems to be from the original text of Ecclesiastes, and it uses "Qohelet" without the definite article, meaning that it is a name.

There are also a number of places where Qohelet is referred to in the third person, beginning with the first two verses:

> RSV1:1 The words of Qohelet, the son of David, king in Jerusalem.
>
> RSV1:2 Vanity of vanities, says Qohelet, vanity of vanities! All is vanity.

The first verse is a very conventional beginning, used in many books of the Bible. For example, the book of Isaiah begins

> Isaiah KJV1:1 The vision of Isaiah the son of Amoz, which he saw concerning Judah and Jerusalem in the days of Uzziah, Jotham, Ahaz, and Hezekiah, kings of Judah..

This sort of beginning is the equivalent of the title page and author biography that publishers add to books today. It is so conventional that it is plausible that the author of *Ecclesiastes* included it in the original book to define the fictional character Qohelet, before quoting the supposed sayings of this character.

Verse 7:27 includes a brief reference to Qohelet in the

third person that seems to have been inserted by a later scribe:

> 7:27 Behold, this have I found, saith (the) Qohelet,
> counting one by one, to find out the account:

In the Hebrew text, "saith Qohelet" is *amarah qohelet*, using the third-person feminine form of the verb (*amarah* rather than *amar*), as if Qohelet were a woman. Why does this book use the feminine form of the verb for a character who is clearly a man? The most likely explanation is that an early scribe added the text *amar haqohelet*, which means, "said the qohelet," using qohelet as a description with the definite article, like "the Preacher." Some later scribe was probably confused by the feminine form of the noun Qohelet and changed the spacing to *amarah qohelet*, using the feminine form of the verb to agree with the noun. (Because Hebrew is written with consonants, these two phrases use the same letters, with the space between words in a different location.) Thus, the Hebrew shows that the scribes who transmitted the book of *Ecclesiastes* themselves were confused by the word *qohelet*.

The final verse that is attributed to Qohelet also says "the Qohelet"

> 12:8 Vanity of vanities, saith the Qohelet; all is vanity.

This indicates that this verse may be a framing device that a scribe added at the end of the sayings attributed to Qohelet, to make all of these sayings seem more like a unified book. This scribe wanted the book to conclude with the same verse that it begins with, to make it seem unified, but he made an error by writing *haqohelet* instead of just *qohelet*, as in the first verse. He was copying a scroll, and it is much more difficult to roll a scroll to see another part of it than it is to leaf through a book to see another page, so he probably worked from memory. Though the text said "Qohelet," he thought of it as "the qohelet": he considered it a description, like "the Preacher" rather than a name.

Though verse 12:8 uses "the qohelet," the epilog beginning in verse 12:9 uses "Qohelet." It seems that the scribe who added the epilog was different from the scribe who added verse 12:8 to make the book seem like a unified whole. The scribe or scribes who added the epilog clearly did think that the book was written by Solomon or some other great sage, as we have seen in the section of the introduction about the epilog, so it is striking that they used "Qohelet" even though "the qohelet" is right there in the previous line. Perhaps by their time, everyone was so certain that *Ecclesiastes* was written by Solomon that scribes thought of both "Qohelet" and "the qohelet" as descriptions, like later translators who translated them both as "Ecclesiastes" in the Septuagint and as "the Preacher" in the King James Version.

The word *qohelet* has been confusing since the days of the early scribes who transmitted *Ecclesiastes*, and names in a similar form were confused in the books of *Ezra* and *Nehemia*. We cannot clarify the meaning of *qohelet* with certainty. We can only say that it most probably was originally meant as the name of a fictional character and was later interpreted as a description of King Solomon.

Changes from the King James Version

This section lists all the changes that this edition makes in the King James Version.

Qohelet

Throughout, this edition replaces "the Preacher" in the King James version with "Qohelet" or with "the Qohelet," for reasons explained above.

Striving after wind

Throughout, this edition replaces "vexation of spirit" in the King James version with "a striving after wind." The Hebrew *ruach* can mean either wind or spirit. The King James version translated *r'ut ruach* as "vexation of spirit," but more recent translations generally recognize that it makes more sense for *ruach* to mean "wind" here. This edition uses the translation from the Revised Standard version, "a striving after wind," which is much more in keeping with Qohelet's basic theme that all is *hevel*, "vanity" or more precisely "vapor" or "a puff of air," and that all our efforts in this world are directed at goals that are insubstantial.

In one location, the King James Version does translate *ruach* as wind:

> KJV5:16b what profit hath he that hath laboured for
> the wind?

This is Qohelet's meaning: we are working for things that are insubstantial and that will ultimately disappear.

I turned

In the King James version, verses 4:1, 4:7, and 9:11 begin with "KJV4:1 So I returned," "KJV4:7 Then I returned," and "KJV9:11 I returned."

In Hebrew, verses 4:1 and 4:7 begin with *v'shavti*, which this edition translates "and I turned," while verse 9:11 begins with *shavti*, which this edition translates "I turned." There is no reason for the King James Version to translate 4:1 and 4:7 differently, since they are the same in Hebrew.

The Hebrew *shavti* literally means "I returned" or "I turned," but here it is being used idiomatically to mean that the speaker is turning to a new subject.

The Revised Standard Version translates *shavti* here as "again," to indicate that it is just the beginning of a new subject, and it does not mean the speaker went to some other place and then returned. However, "again" is weaker than *shavti*, and does not make it clear to the reader that the speaker is beginning a new thought.

Because *shavti* begins several new sections in this edition, it is translated "I turned" to make it very clear that the speaker is using it to begin a new thought. This is not quite idiomatic English, but it does read well because it is so close to the King James "I returned," which many readers are familiar with, and it does not create the possible confusion that the speaker is returning after going to some other place.

Here are examples of the different translations, beginning with the one in this edition:

> 4:1 And I turned, and considered all the oppressions that are done under the sun...."
>
> KJV4:1 So I returned, and considered all the oppressions that are done under the sun
>
> RSV4:1 Again I saw all the oppressions that are practiced under the sun.

This change does not affect the meaning significantly, but it is important structurally. Because *shavti* is a marker of new section in this edition, it is important for the translation to reflect the Hebrew. In this edition, the translation is literal enough to indicate that *v'shavti* is used in 4:1 and 4:7 and *shavti* is used in 9:11. By contrast, the King James Version translates 4:1 and 4:7 differently, while the Revised Standard Version translates all three in the same way as "Again."

2:3a I sought in mine heart to give myself unto wine, still guiding mine heart with wisdom;

The King James version has a very confusing translation of this verse.

> KJV2:3a I sought in mine heart to give myself unto wine, yet acquainting mine heart with wisdom;

The Hebrew *noheg*, translated "acquainting" actually means leading, driving cattle, or guiding. Qohelet is saying here that he tried every way of life so his wisdom could judge which was best, and he still was guided by wisdom in this way even when he tried drunkenness.

The Revised Standard Version changes this verse more drastically than this edition:

> RSV2:3a I searched with my mind how to cheer my body with wine — my mind still guiding me with wisdom

This conveys the meaning, but it is very far from being a literal translation of the Hebrew. The translation in this edition is closer to the Hebrew, makes less of a change in the King James Version, and conveys the meaning clearly.

3:11 He hath made every thing beautiful in its time: also he hath set eternity in their heart, so that no man can find out the work that God maketh from the beginning to the end.

In the King James Version, this verse begins:

> KJV3:11a He hath made every thing beautiful in his time: also he hath set the world in their heart

The Hebrew *ito* can mean either "his time" or "its time." The context makes it clear that Qohelet means each thing is beautiful it its time.

The Hebrew *olam* means either "world" or "eternity." In this case, the meaning clearly should be "eternity."

The point is that everything is beautiful in its time, but God has made man want to understand everything as a whole. In English, "he hath set the world in their heart" gives the impression that God has made man worldly, interested in the things of this world—not that man is interested in understanding everything as a whole.

Most recent translations avoid this misleading use of "the world." For example, the Revised Standard Version translates this verse as:

> RSV3:11a He has made everything beautiful in its time; also he has put eternity into man's mind

Notice that the Revised Standard Version also corrects KJV"beautiful in his time" to RSV"beautiful in its time," as this edition does.

3:14a I know that, whatsoever God doeth, it is for ever: nothing can be added to it, nor any thing taken from it:

The Hebrew *y'hiyeh* is the imperfect tense of to be, which can be either the future or the present tense in Biblical Hebrew. The King James Version translates it as the future:

> KJV3:14a I know that, whatsoever God doeth, it shall be for ever: nothing can be put to it, nor any thing taken from it:

This edition makes it the present, "it is for ever."

The future tense implies that God is acting in history; if God does something at a given time, it will be for ever.

Qohelet's point is that God created the world and no longer acts in history but instead leaves the world to work according to impersonal laws of nature, which cannot be changed. The present tense conveys this idea more clearly.

In addition, this edition changes "put to it" from the King James version to "added to it," because "put to it" was idiomatic English in the seventeenth century but is no longer comprehensible by most English speakers.

The Revised Standard Version translates this verse as:

> RSV3:14 I know that whatever God does endures for ever; nothing can be added to it, nor anything taken from it;

But *y'hiyeh* actually means "is" or "will be," and there is no reason to change it to "endures."

3:18 I said in mine heart concerning the estate of the sons of men, that God is testing them, that they might see that they themselves are beasts.

In the King James Version, this verse is:

> 3:18 I said in mine heart concerning the estate of the sons of men, that God might manifest them, and that they might see that they themselves are beasts.

But the Hebrew *baram*, translated as "manifest," comes from the root *barar*, which means to test. "Manifest" here makes the verse hard for most contemporary English speakers to understand.

5:10 He that loveth money is not satisfied with money; nor he that loveth wealth with increase: this is also vanity.

In the King James Version, this verse is:

> KJV5:10 He that loveth silver shall not be satisfied with silver; nor he that loveth abundance with increase: this is also vanity.

The Hebrew *kesef* can mean either silver or money. Qohelet is talking about the futility of pursuing wealth, as we can see in the earlier verse:

> 4:8 ...there no end of all his labour; neither is his eye satisfied with riches;

The talk about silver and abundance is confusing to the contemporary reader, since we no longer use silver as money and we use "abundance" to mean abundance of all good things rather than just monetary wealth. This edition uses a translation that is more like the Revised Standard Version:

> RSV5:10 He who loves money will not be satisfied with money; nor he who loves wealth, with gain:

In addition, this edition uses the present tense ("is not satisfied") rather than the future ("will not be satisfied"). In Biblical Hebrew, the imperfect tense can be either the present or the future, and the present is more appropriate here, because Qohelet is generalizing, saying that people who love money are not satisfied with their money.

5:20 For he shall not much call to mind the days of his life; because God answereth him in the joy of his heart.

In the King James Version, this verse is translated:

> 5:20 For he shall not much remember the days of his life; because God answereth him in the joy of his heart.

The Hebrew *zachar* is usually used to mean "remember," but it literally means "call to mind." In English, you can only "remember" the past, not the present or the future. In Hebrew, *zachar* can be used with past, present, or future events; it should be translated as "remember" only when it refers to past events.

Here, Qohelet is saying that someone who enjoys the present moment will not think about the fact that the days of his life are numbered. This meaning is lost when *zachar* is translated as "remember."

6:3 If a man beget an hundred children, and live many years, so that the days of his years be many, and he does not enjoy life's good things; I say, that an untimely birth is better than he.

The King James Version translates this as:

> KJV6:3 If a man beget an hundred children, and live many years, so that the days of his years be many, and his soul be not filled with good; and also that he have no burial, I say, that an untimely birth is better than he.

"His soul be filled with good" is an idiom meaning that he enjoys himself. It is misleading to translate it literally, so this edition uses a translation like that of the Revised Standard Version:

> RSV6:3 If a man begets a hundred children, and lives many years, so that the days of his years are many, but he does not enjoy life's good things, ...
>
> I say that an untimely birth is better off than he.

See the section about removed text for an explanation of why this edition removes "and also that he have no burial."

6:3 ...I say, that an untimely birth is better than he.
6:4 For it cometh in with vanity, and departeth in darkness, and its name shall be covered with darkness.
6:5 Moreover it hath not seen the sun, nor known any thing: it has more rest than he.
6:6 Yea, though he live a thousand years twice told, yet hath he seen no good....

The King James Version uses "he" to refer both to the still birth and to the man who cannot enjoy life, making it very difficult to follow:

> 6:3 ...I say, that an untimely birth is better than he.
> 6:4 For he cometh in with vanity, and departeth in darkness, and his name shall be covered with darkness.
> 6:5 Moreover he hath not seen the sun, nor known any thing: this hath more rest than the other.
> 6:6 Yea, though he live a thousand years twice told, yet hath he seen no good....

The Revised Standard Version makes this passage clearer by using "it" to refer to the stillbirth and "he" to refer to the man who cannot enjoy life, and this edition does the same.

6:8 For what hath the wise man more than the fool? what hath the poor man, that knoweth how to conduct himself before the living?

The Hebrew *lahaloch* literally means "to go." The King James Version translates it as "to walk":

> KJV6:8 For what hath the wise more than the fool? what hath the poor, that knoweth to walk before the living?

It is actually being used idiomatically to mean something like "to behave." This edition translates it "to conduct himself," bringing it closer to the Revised Standard Version:

> RSV6:8 For what advantage has the wise man over the fool? And what does the poor man have who knows how to conduct himself before the living?

7:14 In the day of prosperity be joyful, but in the day of adversity consider: God also hath set the one over against the other, to the end that man should not find what is after him.

The King James Version translates this as:

KJV7:14 In the day of prosperity be joyful, but in the day of adversity consider: God also hath set the one over against the other, to the end that man should find nothing after him.

The Hebrew *shelo yimtza ha'adam acharav m'uma* can be translated literally as "should not find after him anything" or "should not find after him what is." The King James Version uses the former translation, which does not make any sense. The latter translation does make sense, as an example of Qohelet's belief that we cannot understand God's work completely.

Most modern translations use a variation on the latter translation, as this edition does. For example, the Revised Standard Version says:

RSV7:14 In the day of prosperity be joyful, and in the day of adversity consider; God has made the one as well as the other, so that man may not find out anything that will be after him.

8:6 Because to every purpose there is time and judgment, although the misery of man is great upon him.

The King James Version translates this verse using "therefore" instead of "although":

8:6 Because to every purpose there is time and judgment, therefore the misery of man is great upon him.

The Hebrew word is *ki*, which is a connective that can be used in many ways. It is most often translated as "for," indicating that the new thought follows from what preceeded, but in Biblical Hebrew, it can also be translated "but," indicating that the new thought is the opposite of what you would expect from what preceded.

In this case, the context seems to indicate that the new thought is the opposite of what you would expect, so this edition translates *ki* as "although" rather than as "therefore." The Revised Standard Version does the same, translating this verse as:

> RSV8:6 For every matter has its time and way, although man's trouble lies heavy upon him.

The meaning is that everything is good in its time, although attempting to understand everything makes us unhappy.

8:7 For he knoweth not that which shall be: for who can tell him?

The King James Version says:

> KJV8:7 For he knoweth not that which shall be: for who can tell him when it shall be?

The Revised Standard Version says:

> RSV8:7 For he does not know what is to be, for who can tell him how it will be?

The Hebrew verse ends *mi yagid lo*, which simply means "who will tell him," and we have translated this phrase literally.

8:15 Then I commended mirth, because a man hath no better thing under the sun, than to eat, and to drink, and to be merry: for that shall abide with him in his labour the days of his life, which God giveth him under the sun.

This edition makes a minor change from the King James Version, which translates

> KJV8:15 …of his labour…

instead of "in his labor."

The Hebrew is *ba'amalo*, and the prefix *b'* generally means "in." The translation "in" also makes much more sense in terms of Qohelet's view of the world: he is saying that enjoyment will stay with you while you are laboring all your life.

9:1 For all this I considered in my heart even to declare all this, that the righteous, and the wise, and their works, are in the hand of God: man knoweth not all that is before them, love or hatred.

This is a difficult verse to translate. The King James Version translates it in a way that does not make much sense:

> KJV9:1 … the righteous, and the wise, and their works, are in the hand of God: no man knoweth either love or hatred by all that is before them.

The Revised Standard Version makes a bit more sense

> RSV9:1 the righteous and the wise and their deeds are in the hand of God; whether it is love or hate

> man does not know. Everything before them is vanity.

but it adds, "Everything before them is vanity," which is nowhere in the original.

In Hebrew, the second part of the verse is:

> *gam ahava gam sin'ah eyn yodea ha'adam hakol lifneyhem*

which literally means:

> Also love also hatred does not know the man all before them.

The word *gam* is just used as a transition, and this edition leaves it out and translates the rest of the passage literally, using the archaic "knoweth not" to match the language of the King James translation in nearby verses.

The meaning, of course, is that it is not necessarily true that good things happen to the righteous; their fate may turn out as if God loved them and may turn out as if God hated them.

10:8 He that diggeth a pit may fall into it; and he that breaketh a wall, a serpent may bite him.

10:9 He that removeth stones may be hurt therewith; and he that cleaveth wood may be endangered thereby.

The King James Version translates these verses as:

> KJV10:8 He that diggeth a pit shall fall into it; and whoso breaketh an hedge, a serpent shall bite him.

> KJV10:9 Whoso removeth stones shall be hurt therewith; and he that cleaveth wood shall be endangered thereby.

The verbs are in the imperfect tense in Hebrew, which is usually translated as the indicative (as in the King James Version) but which can also be used to express possibility.

In this case, the context makes it clear that they express possibility. Qohelet is giving illustrations of the point that begins this section:

> 9:11 ... that the race is not to the swift, nor the battle to the strong, neither yet bread to the wise, nor yet riches to men of understanding, nor yet favour to men of skill; but time and chance happeneth to them all.

In these cases, too, the result is a matter of chance: if you split wood, for example, a piece may go flying and hit you. Of course, it makes no sense to say with certainty that a piece of wood will go flying and hit you.

In a couple of places in these verses, the King James Version uses "whoso," which means "whoever." Since it just indicates possibility, this edition replaces "whoso" with "he that," to be consistent with the other examples in these verses.

In verse 10:8, the King James Version translates *gader* as "hedge," but its literal meaning is "wall" or "fence." The image is of someone breaking up a stone wall and being bitten by a snake that lives in a crack between the stones, so this edition translates as "wall" rather than "hedge."

The Anchor Bible gets the meaning right in its translation of these verses:

> ANC10:8 One who digs a pit may fall into it; and one who breaks down a wall may be bitten by a snake.
>
> ANC 10:9 One who quarries stones may be injured by them, one who splits logs may be endangered by them.

10:11 If the serpent bites before it is charmed, there is no advantage for the charmer.

The King James Version translates this verse as:

> KJV10:11 Surely the serpent will bite without enchantment; and a babbler is no better.

This is simply an error. The Hebrew *ba'al halashon* literally means "the master of the tongue." The King James Version translates this as "babbler," but it actually means "charmer," someone who is a master of the spells that can charm the snake.

The Revised Standard Version does better:

> RSV10:11 If the serpent bites before it is charmed, there is no advantage in a charmer.

but the Hebrew says *l'ba'al halashon*, which means "to the charmer" or "for the charmer." This edition translated this phrase literally.

This verse is another example of how chance can outweigh skill. Even if the snake charmer is skilled, the snake may bite him before he has time to charm it.

10:19 A feast is made for laughter, and wine maketh merry, and money answereth all things.

This edition changes the word "but" to "and" in the verse:

> KJV10:19 A feast is made for laughter, and wine maketh merry: but money answereth all things.

The Hebrew prefix v' can be translated as either "and" or "but" in Biblical Hebrew.

Here, it is more appropriate to translate it as "and." This verse is another example of Qohelet's belief that we should enjoy the things of this world: a feast, wine, and money are three of those things. The word "but" implies that there is a contrast between the feast and wine and the money, which is not the case here.

Unchanged from the King James Version

This section lists a couple of cases where this edition retains the translation of the King James Version, though this translation might be controversial.

Vanity

The King James Version uses the word "vanity" in an archaic sense. Normally, it is best to make a translation clearer by replacing archaic words with contemporary words that the reader is more likely to understand, but its use in *Ecclesiastes* has become such a part of the English language that it would be jarring to replace it. Changing

1:2 ... vanity of vanities; all is vanity

would be like editing Shakespeare to make Juliet say, "Romeo, Romeo, why are you Romeo?"

9:10 ... for there is no work, nor device, nor knowledge, nor wisdom, in the grave, whither thou goest.

This edition keeps the translation "the grave" from the King James Version. In Hebrew, the word is *she'ol,*

She'ol is the world of the dead in the ancient Israelite religion, a place of darkness filled with shades that have no strength or personality, where all people go after death, whether they were righteous or unrighteous.

Qohelet makes it clear in many places that the conventional religion of his time, which he can no longer believe, has a view of the afterlife that is much more like the modern Jewish and Christian view. For example, he says:

> 3:19 For that which befalleth the sons of men befalleth beasts; even one thing befalleth them: as the one dieth, so dieth the other; yea, they have all one breath; so that a man hath no preeminence above a beast: for all is vanity.
>
> 3:20 All go unto one place; all are of the dust, and all turn to dust again.
>
> 3:21 Who knoweth the spirit of man that goeth upward, and the spirit of the beast that goeth downward to the earth?

Here, he is rejecting the conventional religion of his time, which says that the spirits of men go up to heaven after death; instead, he believes that men just turn to dust after death. Throughout the book, his point is that the human spirit simply disappears after death.

Some translations leave the Hebrew word *she'ol* in this verse. For example, the Revised Standard Version says:

> RSV9:10 there is no work or thought or knowledge or wisdom in Sheol, to which you are going.

but this archaic view of the afterlife is completely alien to the point that Qohelet makes throughout this book.

The best explanation is that Qohelet is using *she'ol* here as a euphemism for death, and that he expected his readers to understand it in this way. Keeping the word *she'ol* in the translation misleads the contemporary reader into thinking that Qohelet believed in an archaic version of the Israelite religion, while the entire book shows that he was actually rejecting a later version of the Jewish religion in favor of a more materialistic view of the world.

Removed Text

This section lists all of the passages that this edition removes from the received text of *Ecclesiastes* to restore its original text, with the reason for removing each.

²:²⁴ ... This also I saw, that it was from the hand of God.
²:²⁵ **For who can eat, or who else can hasten hereunto, more than I?**
²:²⁶ **For God giveth to a man that is good in his sight wisdom, and knowledge, and joy: but to the sinner he giveth travail, to gather and to heap up, that he may give to him that is good before God. This also is vanity and a striving after wind.**

Qohelet has just given up on his attempts to understand the purpose of life and has decided that it is best to live in the present, saying:

> ²:²⁴ There is nothing better for a man, than that he should eat and drink, and that he should make his soul enjoy good in his labour.

The editor inserts this passage that moralizes Qohelet's decision by saying that the ability to live in the present is a result of God's justice: he gives this ability to good people but not to sinners. This discovery of God's justice in the world is just the opposite of what Qohelet says throughout the book. This passage makes "vanity and a striving after wind" apply only to the sinners who cannot enjoy life because God is punishing them, while Qohelet clearly means it to apply more generally.

3:17 I said in mine heart, God shall judge the righteous and the wicked: for there is a time there for every purpose and for every work.

This verse says the opposite of the verses that surround it:

> 3:16 And moreover I saw under the sun the place of judgment, that wickedness was there; and the place of righteousness, that iniquity was there.
>
> 3:18 I said in mine heart concerning the estate of the sons of men, that God is testing them, that they might see that they themselves are beasts.
>
> 3:19 For that which befalleth the sons of men befalleth beasts; even one thing befalleth them: as the one dieth, so dieth the other; yea, they have all one breath; so that a man hath no pre-eminence above a beast: for all is vanity.

One of Qohelet's key points throughout is that there is no justice in the world, as far as we can see. He is illustrating that point in this passage, but a later scribe added verse 3:17 saying the opposite, that there is justice after all.

⁴:⁸ There is one alone, and there is not a second; yea, he hath neither child nor brother: yet is there no end of all his labour; neither is his eye satisfied with riches; neither saith he, For whom do I labour, and bereave my soul of good? This is also vanity, yea, it is a sore travail.

⁴:⁹ Two are better than one; because they have a good reward for their labour.

⁴:¹⁰ For if they fall, the one will lift up his fellow: but woe to him that is alone when he falleth; for he hath not another to help him up.

⁴:¹¹ Again, if two lie together, then they have heat: but how can one be warm alone?

⁴:¹² And if one prevail against him, two shall withstand him; and a threefold cord is not quickly broken.

Qohelet is about to say that it is worthless to have money if you cannot enjoy it, continuing his theme that we should enjoy the moment, but the scribe inserts conventional ideas about the advantage of not being alone, ending with a proverb. These verses are not related to Qohelet's theme, that there are people who pursue riches and are never satisfied.

⁴:¹³ Better is a poor and a wise child than an old and foolish king, who will no more be admonished.

⁴:¹⁴ For out of prison he cometh to reign; whereas also he that is born in his kingdom becometh poor.

⁴:¹⁵ I considered all the living which walk under the sun, with the second child that shall stand up in his stead.

4:16 There is no end of all the people, even of all that have been before them: they also that come after shall not rejoice in him. Surely this also is vanity and a striving after wind.

Again, the scribe inserts conventional ideas about the value of wisdom.

5:1 Keep thy foot when thou goest to the house of God, and be more ready to hear, than to give the sacrifice of fools: for they consider not that they do evil.

5:2 Be not rash with thy mouth, and let not thine heart be hasty to utter any thing before God: for God is in heaven, and thou upon earth: therefore let thy words be few.

5:3 For a dream cometh through the multitude of business; and a fool's voice is known by multitude of words.

5:4 When thou vowest a vow unto God, defer not to pay it; for he hath no pleasure in fools: pay that which thou hast vowed.

5:5 Better is it that thou shouldest not vow, than that thou shouldest vow and not pay.

5:6 Suffer not thy mouth to cause thy flesh to sin; neither say thou before the angel, that it was an error: wherefore should God be angry at thy voice, and destroy the work of thine hands?

5:7 For in the multitude of dreams and many words there are also divers vanities: but fear thou God.

5:8 If thou seest the oppression of the poor, and violent perverting of judgment and justice in a province, marvel

not at the matter: for he that is higher than the highest regardeth; and there be higher than they.

5:9 Moreover the profit of the earth is for all: the king himself is served by the field.

These verses praise conventional forms of piety, listening when you go to the house of God, keeping your vows, and not criticizing others.

The last two verses look at the theme of injustice by government officials, which concerns Qohelet, but they give reasons for not being upset by injustice, as Qohelet is: there are higher officials overseeing the lower officials who are unjust, and at any rate, it is an advantage for a land to have a king and government. The final verse is better translated in the Revised Standard Version as:

RSV5:9 But in all, a king is an advantage to a land
with cultivated fields.

5:14 But those riches perish by evil travail: and he begetteth a son, and there is nothing in his hand.

"Evil travail" is misleading to the modern reader, and the Revised Standard Version clarifies the beginning of this verse:

RSV5:14 and those riches were lost in a bad venture;
and he is father of a son, but he has nothing in his
hand.

This verse gives a more conventional explanation of the point that Qohelet is making in the passage where it is inserted:

> 5:13 There is a sore evil which I have seen under the sun, namely, riches kept for the owners thereof to their hurt.
>
> 5:15 As he came forth of his mother's womb, naked shall he return to go as he came, and shall take nothing of his labour, which he may carry away in his hand.

Qohelet repeatedly makes the point that some people never enjoy their lives because they are consumed with pursuing riches, and so they inevitably die without ever benefiting from these riches.

The scribe who inserted this verse added the explanation that a rich man might lose his money and not be able to support his son, which has nothing to do with Qohelet's point.

6:3 ...and also that he have no burial...

Just this phrase is removed from verse 6:3:

> 6:3 If a man beget an hundred children, and live many years, so that the days of his years be many, and he does not enjoy life's good things, and also that he have no burial; I say, that an untimely birth is better than he.

Qohelet is saying in this section that it is better not to be born than to be rich and successful without enjoying your riches. A scribe has inserted a more pious explanation: it is better not to be born if you do not have a proper burial.

6:10 That which hath been is named already, and it is known that it is man: neither may he contend with him that is mightier than he.

6:11 Seeing there be many things that increase vanity, what is man the better?

This text is problematic, as we can see by comparing the above translation from the King James Version with the Revised Standard Version:

> RSV6:10 Whatever has come to be has already been named, and it is known what man is, and that he is not able to dispute with one stronger than he.
>
> RSV6:11 The more words, the more vanity, and what is man the better?

And with the Anchor Bible:

> ANC6:10 Whatever happens has already been designated; the course of human beings is known, and they cannot dispute with the one who is stronger than they.
>
> ANC6:11 Indeed, there are many words that increase vanity. What advantage do human beings have?

The Hebrew text is probably corrupt, and there have been many different attempts to revise it so the passage makes more sense.

It seems like a disruption between the surrounding verses, which make perfect sense in sequence, without this difficult passage between them:

> 6:9 Better is the sight of the eyes than the wandering of the desire: this is also vanity and a striving after wind.

6:12 For who knoweth what is good for man in this life, all the days of his vain life which he spendeth as a shadow? for who can tell a man what shall be after him under the sun?

Some future correction of these verses might make it clear that they are part of the original text, but until then, it is best to remove them to make the original text more readable.

7:1 **A good name is better than precious ointment; and the day of death than the day of one's birth.**

7:2 **It is better to go to the house of mourning, than to go to the house of feasting: for that is the end of all men; and the living will lay it to his heart.**

7:3 **Sorrow is better than laughter: for by the sadness of the countenance the heart is made better.**

7:4 **The heart of the wise is in the house of mourning; but the heart of fools is in the house of mirth.**

7:5 **It is better to hear the rebuke of the wise, than for a man to hear the song of fools.**

7:6 **For as the crackling of thorns under a pot, so is the laughter of the fool: this also is vanity.**

7:7 **Surely oppression maketh a wise man mad; and a gift destroyeth the heart.**

7:8 **Better is the end of a thing than the beginning thereof: and the patient in spirit is better than the proud in spirit.**

The Revised Standard Version clarifies Verse 7:7 as:

RSV7:7 Surely oppression makes the wise man foolish,
and a bribe corrupts the mind.

Since the imperfect can either be the indicative or can express possibility (as we have seen), the verse can also be translated as:

7:7 Surely oppression may make the wise man foolish, and a bribe may corrupt the mind.

Here, the scribe has inserted a fairly long text that says we should always be mindful of our inevitable death rather than enjoying this life. If we remember our end, we will patiently endure the suffering and temptations of this world. Of course, this is just the opposite of Qohelet's attitude that we should try our best to enjoy life and not to think about our death.

7:9 Be not hasty in thy spirit to be angry: for anger resteth in the bosom of fools.

7:10 Say not thou, What is the cause that the former days were better than these? for thou dost not inquire wisely concerning this.

7:11 Wisdom is good with an inheritance: and by it there is profit to them that see the sun.

7:12 For wisdom is a defence, and money is a defence: but the excellency of knowledge is, that wisdom giveth life to them that have it.

The scribe inserts conventional ideas about folly and wisdom.

7:18 It is good that thou shouldest take hold of this; yea, also from this withdraw not thine hand: for he that feareth God shall come forth of them all.

7:19 Wisdom strengtheneth the wise more than ten mighty men which are in the city.

Again, the scribe inserts conventional ideas about fear of God and wisdom.

7:21 Also take no heed unto all words that are spoken; lest thou hear thy servant curse thee:

7:22 For oftentimes also thine own heart knoweth that thou thyself likewise hast cursed others.

This text is problematic. It could be seen as another example of the theme of the preceding verse, that no man is perfectly righteous.

> 7:20 For there is not a just man upon earth, that doeth good, and sinneth not.

However, it does not seem to continue the thought of the earlier verses:

> 7:15 All things have I seen in the days of my vanity: there is a just man that perisheth in his righteousness, and there is a wicked man that prolongeth his life in his wickedness.
>
> 7:16 Be not righteous over much; neither make thyself over wise: why shouldest thou destroy thyself?
>
> 7:17 Be not over much wicked, neither be thou foolish: why shouldest thou die before thy time?

The advice that it begins with, "7:21 Also take no heed unto all words that are spoken..." seems unrelated to the surrounding verses, and the remaining text is clearer if we treat these two verses as a later addition.

7:26 And I find more bitter than death the woman, whose heart is snares and nets, and her hands as bands: whoso pleaseth God shall escape from her; but the sinner shall be taken by her.

The complaint about woman in the first half of this verse is unrelated to what Qohelet is saying here. The claim that this type of woman punishes the sinner but not the righteous is just the opposite of Qohelet's point this world is not just.

This verse may be a proverb that refers to the fear of marrying foreign women, who may lead one away from Judaism.

7:27 ... saith [the] Qohelet

This edition just removes "saith the preacher" from this verse of the King James Version:

KJV7:27 Behold, this have I found, saith the preacher,

counting one by one, to find out the account:

Here, "saith the preacher" translates the Hebrew *amarh qohelet*, which uses the feminine form of the verb. The section "Qohelet and the Qohelet" discusses why this was inserted and then misunderstood by later scribes.

7:28b one man among a thousand have I found; but a woman among all those have I not found.
7:29 Lo, this only have I found, that God hath made man upright; but they have sought out many inventions.

The first of these two verses continues the anti-woman verse that was inserted two verses earlier. The second is the opposite of Qohelet's opinion:

> **7:13** Consider the work of God: for who can make that straight, which he hath made crooked?

8:1 Who is as the wise man? and who knoweth the interpretation of a thing? a man's wisdom maketh his face to shine, and the boldness of his face shall be changed.
8:2 I counsel thee to keep the king's commandment, and that in regard of the oath of God.
8:3 Be not hasty to go out of his sight: stand not in an evil thing; for he doeth whatsoever pleaseth him.
8:4 Where the word of a king is, there is power: and who may say unto him, What doest thou?
8:5 Whoso keepeth the commandment shall feel no evil thing: and a wise man's heart discerneth both time and judgment.

These verses begin with conventional ideas in praise of wisdom and continue with conventional ideas about obeying authority.

8:8 There is no man that hath power over the spirit to retain the spirit; neither hath he power in the day of death: and there is no discharge in that war; neither shall wickedness deliver those that are given to it.

Qohelet was making his usual point that we cannot understand our lives as a whole:

8:7 For he knoweth not that which shall be: for who can tell him?

A scribe inserted this verse with the conventional sentiment that we cannot know when we die and that the wicked should fear what will happen to them after death.

8:11 Because sentence against an evil work is not executed speedily, therefore the heart of the sons of men is fully set in them to do evil.
8:12 Though a sinner do evil an hundred times, and his days be prolonged, yet surely I know that it shall be well with them that fear God, which fear before him:
8:13 But it shall not be well with the wicked, neither shall he prolong his days, which are as a shadow; because he feareth not before God.

These three verses contain conventional ideas. The final two of them are just the opposite of Qohelet's point that the world is unjust because the wicked sometimes prosper.

Incidentally, verse 8:11 contains Persian loan word, *pitgam*, which is translated as "sentence." Many scholars use both *pitgam* here and *pardesim* in verse 2:5 as decisive proof that *Ecclesiastes* was written much later than the time of Solomon. Because this edition does not include this verse as part of the original book of *Ecclesiastes*, the introduction just uses *pardesim* to show that *Ecclesiastes* must have been written after there was Persian influence on Hebrew.

9:14 There was a little city, and few men within it; and there came a great king against it, and besieged it, and built great bulwarks against it:

9:15 Now there was found in it a poor wise man, and he by his wisdom delivered the city; yet no man remembered that same poor man.

9:16 Then said I, Wisdom is better than strength: nevertheless the poor man's wisdom is despised, and his words are not heard.

9:17 The words of wise men are heard in quiet more than the cry of him that ruleth among fools.

9:18 Wisdom is better than weapons of war: but one sinner destroyeth much good.

10:1 Dead flies cause the ointment of the apothecary to send forth a stinking savour: so doth a little folly him that is in reputation for wisdom and honour.

10:2 A wise man's heart is at his right hand; but a fool's heart at his left.

10:3 Yea also, when he that is a fool walketh by the way, his wisdom faileth him, and he saith to every one that he is a fool.

10:4 If the spirit of the ruler rise up against thee, leave not thy place; for yielding pacifieth great offences.

10:5 There is an evil which I have seen under the sun, as an error which proceedeth from the ruler:

10:6 Folly is set in great dignity, and the rich sit in low place.

10:7 I have seen servants upon horses, and princes walking as servants upon the earth.

This text begins with a parable that illustrates the conventional wisdom that wisdom is better than power

The final three verses are interesting, because they complain that the world is not ordered properly, as Qohelet often does, but for a very different reason. Qohelet complains that the world is unjust, that people are oppressed, that fools prosper. These verses complain that conventional social status is ignored: the rich should be in a high place, and princes should be above slaves.

The translation of the first three of these verses is problematic. As we have seen, the imperfect can be used either as an indicative or to express possibility, and the word *zachar*, which is usually translated "remember," actually means "call to mind" and should be translated "remember" only when it refers to the past. Thus, verse 9:13 could be translated differently, so these three verses would be:

> 9:14 There was a little city, and few men within it; and there came a great king against it, and besieged it, and built great bulwarks against it:

9:15 Now there was found in it a poor wise man, and he by his wisdom could have delivered the city; yet no man called to mind that same poor man.

9:16 Then said I, Wisdom is better than strength: nevertheless the poor man's wisdom is despised, and his words are not heard.

This revised translation of 9:15 makes more sense. Verse 9:16 says that the poor man's words are not heard. Verse 9:15 in the King James Version says that the poor man delivered the city, which implies that his words were heard, though he was forgotten afterwards.

With this revised translation, these three verses might fit into the original text of *Ecclesiastes*, as an illustration of the point in the surrounding verses that wisdom does not always succeed. However, it has been removed because the translation is problematic and including it seems to make the text as a whole less coherent.

10:10 If the iron be blunt, and he do not whet the edge, then must he put to more strength: but wisdom is profitable to direct.

This verse is a conventional praise of wisdom that says just the opposite of the preceding verses:

10:8 He that diggeth a pit may fall into it; and he that breaketh a wall, a serpent may bite him.

10:9 He that removeth stones may be hurt therewith; and he that cleaveth wood may be endangered thereby.

10:11 If the serpent bites before it is charmed, there is no advantage for the charmer.

These surrounding verses say that chance may foil someone who is doing his work. For example, someone who is doing the routine job of breaking up a stone wall to reuse the stones may be bitten by a snake that is living in the spaces between the stones; and if someone is splitting wood, a piece may fly off and hit him.

By contrast, this verse says that wisdom lets you avoid this sort of problem. For example, if you are using a blunt tool, you are more likely to have problems (like someone who uses a blunt axe to split wood), but if you are wise, you will sharpen the tool and avoid these problems.

Qohelet is saying that our lives are ruled by chance, regardless of our skill, and a scribe inserted this verse to say that, if we are wise, we can have some control over chance.

10:12 The words of a wise man's mouth are gracious; but the lips of a fool will swallow up himself.

10:13 The beginning of the words of his mouth is foolishness: and the end of his talk is mischievous madness.

10:14 A fool also is full of words: a man cannot tell what shall be; and what shall be after him, who can tell him?

10:15 The labour of the foolish wearieth every one of them, because he knoweth not how to go to the city.

10:16 Woe to thee, O land, when thy king is a child, and thy princes eat in the morning!

10:17 Blessed art thou, O land, when thy king is the son of nobles, and thy princes eat in due season, for strength, and not for drunkenness!

10:18 By much slothfulness the building decayeth; and through idleness of the hands the house droppeth through.

These verses are conventional praise of wisdom and temperance, and they also support the conventional social order.

10:20 Curse not the king, no not in thy thought; and curse not the rich in thy bedchamber: for a bird of the air shall carry the voice, and that which hath wings shall tell the matter.

This is another verse that supports the conventional social order.

11:1 Cast thy bread upon the waters: for thou shalt find it after many days.

11:2 Give a portion to seven, and also to eight; for thou knowest not what evil shall be upon the earth.

These verses are problematic. In this translation, they sound like conventionally pious advice, saying that we should do good because we will ultimately be rewarded for it.

However, the imperfect in Biblical Hebrew is usually used as the indicative but can also be used to express possibility, as we have seen, so the first of these verses could also be translated:

> 11:1 Cast thy bread upon the waters: for thou mayst find it after many days.

With this revision, these two verses have a similar meaning to the nearby verse:

> 11:6 In the morning sow thy seed, and in the evening withhold not thine hand: for thou knowest not whether shall prosper, either this or that, or whether they both shall be alike good.

In both cases, Qohelet is giving us the practical advice that we should try a number of different things, because we do not know that any one will be successful.

However, verses 11:1 and 11:2 are not located where they fit into the sequence of ideas in this section, so the text is more coherent and more readable if they are removed.

11:9 Rejoice, O young man, in thy youth; and let thy heart cheer thee in the days of thy youth, and walk in the ways of thine heart, and in the sight of thine eyes: but know thou, that for all these things God will bring thee into judgment.

11:10 Therefore remove sorrow from thy heart, and put away evil from thy flesh: for childhood and youth are vanity.

¹²⁻¹ Remember now thy Creator in the days of thy youth, while the evil days come not, nor the years draw nigh, when thou shalt say, I have no pleasure in them;

¹²⁻² While the sun, or the light, or the moon, or the stars, be not darkened, nor the clouds return after the rain:

¹²⁻³ In the day when the keepers of the house shall tremble, and the strong men shall bow themselves, and the grinders cease because they are few, and those that look out of the windows be darkened,

¹²⁻⁴ And the doors shall be shut in the streets, when the sound of the grinding is low, and he shall rise up at the voice of the bird, and all the daughters of musick shall be brought low;

¹²⁻⁵ Also when they shall be afraid of that which is high, and fears shall be in the way, and the almond tree shall flourish, and the grasshopper shall be a burden, and desire shall fail: because man goeth to his long home, and the mourners go about the streets:

¹²⁻⁶ Or ever the silver cord be loosed, or the golden bowl be broken, or the pitcher be broken at the fountain, or the wheel broken at the cistern.

¹²⁻⁷ Then shall the dust return to the earth as it was: and the spirit shall return unto God who gave it.

This beautiful poem tells us to enjoy our youth but also to remember our creator during our youth, because death will come and our spirit will return to God. It includes a long series of moving metaphors for extreme old age and death. Its point is just the opposite of Qohelet's belief that we return to dust after death:

3:19 For that which befalleth the sons of men befalleth beasts; even one thing befalleth them: as the one dieth, so dieth the other; yea, they have all one breath; so that a man hath no pre-eminence above a beast: for all is vanity.

3:20 All go unto one place; all are of the dust, and all turn to dust again.

12:8 **Vanity of vanities, saith the Qohelet; all is vanity.**

This verse says "the Qohelet" rather than "Qohelet," indicating that it was probably added by a scribe, who intended it to be a framing device, as discussed in the section on "Qohelet and the Qohelet." The scribe tried to make the book seem like a coherent whole by rounding it off with a verse at the end that repeats the beginning.

With this verse removed, the ending in this edition is more effective:

> 11:7 Truly the light is sweet, and a pleasant thing it is for the eyes to behold the sun:
>
> 11:8 But if a man live many years, and rejoice in them all; yet let him remember the days of darkness; for they shall be many. All that cometh is vanity.

Rather than just repeating the beginning verse, it refers to both the beginning verse and to the reconciliation that Qohelet has developed throughout the book, making it clear that the reconciliation is only partial.

12:9 And moreover, because Qohelet was wise, he still taught the people knowledge; yea, he gave good heed, and sought out, and set in order many proverbs.

12:10 Qohelet sought to find out acceptable words: and that which was written was upright, even words of truth.

12:11 The words of the wise are as goads, and as nails fastened by the masters of assemblies, which are given from one shepherd.

12:12 And further, by these, my son, be admonished: of making many books there is no end; and much study is a weariness of the flesh.

12:13 Let us hear the conclusion of the whole matter: Fear God, and keep his commandments: for this is the whole duty of man.

12:14 For God shall bring every work into judgment, with every secret thing, whether it be good, or whether it be evil.

This epilog is explicitly by the scribe (or scribes) rather than by Qohelet. It assumes that Qohelet was a great sage rather than a fictional character, and it tries to mitigate any ill effects of Qohelet's unorthodox advice, as discussed in the introduction.

www.ingramcontent.com/pod-product-compliance
Lightning Source LLC
Chambersburg PA
CBHW030003050426
42451CB00006B/95